Personal Transformation

Techniques to Stay Focused, Overcome Distractions, and Achieve Goals

Benjamin Brayshaw

Table of Contents

Disclaimer

This book has been written for information purposes only. Every effort has been made to make this book as complete and accurate as possible. However, there may be mistakes in typography or content. Also, this book provides information only up to the publishing date. Therefore, this book should be a guide, not the ultimate source.

The purpose of this book is to educate. The author and the publisher do not warrant that the information contained in this book is fully complete and shall not be responsible for any errors or omissions. The author and publisher shall have neither liability nor responsibility to any person or entity with respect to any loss or damage caused or alleged to be caused directly or indirectly by this book.

Chapter 1
How To Motivate Yourself

You may learn to be more motivated by reading many motivation-related articles, books, and blog posts. They often provide advice such as "Get more sleep" and "Introduce new Habits Slowly."

All of these concepts have some value, but ultimately they fall short. This technique won't immediately make you more focused if you have trouble staying motivated and focusing on new projects.

And how are you supposed to maintain the improvements that result in more motivation if you find it difficult to inspire yourself? Don't you feel like it's kind of a vicious circle?

You need to go further if you truly want to see improvements. You should concentrate on the real neurology that supports our capacity to become and maintain motivation. In this article, you'll uncover the precise molecular mechanisms behind motivation and, more significantly, how to control those mechanisms for your purposes.

Introducing the Salience Network

What neuroscientists and psychologists refer to as "attentional control" or "executive function" is what we're interested in here.

Attention. This expresses our capacity to concentrate and maintain our attention and our ability to decide what to pay attention to and disregard.

How, then, does this operate? Many frontal lobes in the brain primarily control this function. The anterior cingulate cortex is perhaps the most renowned product of many studies.

However, two distinct networks of brain regions—areas that cooperate to produce the intended outcome—control attention. These networks are known as the "ventral attention network" (which runs along the bottom) and the "dorsal attention network," which contains brain areas that run along the top of the brain (dorsal means "top" in biology, thus "dorsal fin").

Understanding these two distinct attention networks is essential because they provide distinct functions that reveal how to focus attention better. The dorsal attention network—a bit of a tongue twister—is focused on our purposeful attention. In other words, you are utilizing the dorsal network whether you decide to check the clock or concentrate on a book for a long time.

In contrast, the ventral attention network is activated when our attention is reflexively drawn in an uncontrollable direction. In other words, your ventral attention network is activated when you hear a big boom and turn to gaze at it.

But various other biological cues may potentially divert your ventral attention network. For example, if you are hungry, your ventral attention network will start to drive your attention toward acquiring food. If you are weary, it will direct your attention in that direction.

Therefore, it will be difficult to focus if you're attempting to get work done and other things keep drawing it away.

The next thing we need to investigate is how the brain chooses what to focus on. The salience network', a different neural network, provides the solution. This network informs us what matters and what doesn't, and it seems intimately related to our capacity for self-motivation.

In other words, those who can communicate to their brains what is essential can concentrate on their task, run further, and maintain a high concentration level while competing.

But what can you do to change the situation if you weren't endowed with a powerful salience network from birth?

Regaining Control

What is the salience network's functioning? What does it consider to be crucial?

The explanation is based on the course of human evolution. Our psyche has developed in the ways that it has for our survival in every manner. Characteristics that were helpful to our long-term survival would be handed down to our progeny, while detrimental characteristics would gradually disappear.

As a result, this network's role is to warn us about

situations crucial to our survival. It does this by using connections we have made and biochemical signals from our bodies. When you see a lion, your salience network will recognize it as something significant, activating the ventral attention network and focusing your attention there.

Your parasympathetic nervous system will activate, causing a hormonal and neurochemical reaction. You will create adrenaline, dopamine, cortisol, and norepinephrine, and these chemicals will cause your heart rate to increase, cause your muscles to contract, and cause you to focus just on that one item.

This also occurs to a lesser amount whether you are hungry, too hot, too cold, or anxious about another issue, such as debt, a relationship, or anything else.

Therefore, the first step in improving your capacity to concentrate and maintain motivation is eliminating distractions that interfere with your dorsal attention network. This implies that you must set up a workspace that is both distraction-free and as pleasant as you can manage.

Any loud noise, pain, hunger, or persistent tension might make staying focused difficult.

The founder of WordPress, Matt Mullenweg, shared a tip you may adopt to promote a more focused mental state. During a podcast with Tim Ferriss, he explained how he would repeatedly play familiar music. He would hear the song again and become very used to it. The brain would then begin to phase that music out as a consequence. In other words, as you ultimately cease hearing the clock's ticking, it would get numb. It will only completely mask other sounds if you use headphones while listening to the music.

As a result, a kind of sensory deprivation is successfully created. The brain fully muffles the one sound that is present. White noise may help you accomplish a similar goal, and many individuals use it to help them concentrate while working. Other harmless noises, such as the rain or background talk, are similar to white noise. Both the website Rainymood.com and the website Coffitivity.com provide similar looping videos.

Enabling you to filter out your environment with noises. Similarly to this, employing a widescreen display may aid in maintaining your level of concentration at work. According to studies, Widescreen displays have been shown to boost productivity by up to 30%.

However, attempting to rid your thoughts of every other tension is the most crucial thing you can do. Thus, you should strive to quit thinking about your debt and even the other tasks you must do that day. If you are concerned about such things, your attention will wander from the task. To concentrate only on the work, try to learn to shut off sensations of worry and anxiety. The more you train your mind, the more control you will have over it. This may take some effort, but it operates much like a muscle.

Jedi Mind Tricks

But if we want to regulate our drive fully, we must go further than this. We need to make sure that our dorsal and ventral attention networks are coordinated. Where do we start?

The cause of our initial distraction is where the solution resides. We believe that what we should be doing is not only not essential but that other things are more important. You may know you must tidy up, go to the gym, or clean the home. Your dorsal network is working there.

Your body, however, is unaware of that. This dull

exercise doesn't further any of your primary objectives in your body. Our brains need stimulation, which is correlated with the neuronal activity that results from doing tasks that seem to be of biological importance. This is why watching or playing computer games or movies allows us to concentrate easily—they replicate thrilling, significant events that are all emotionally charged.

Nevertheless, entering data into a spreadsheet? Not really.

However, our intellect derives from our capacity to concentrate on what we need to do rather than merely what is now essential to us physiologically.

Be doing in the future. In other words, what has made humans so extraordinarily successful is our capacity for extrapolation, planning, and prediction.

This results from our working memory, which is the capacity to retain information mentally. The brain may be trained to concentrate on events that have already occurred or those we anticipate will occur, making it seem like they are occurring. Our vision consists of internalizing our experience to control the variables.

Learning to connect the tedious task or activity you

don't want to undertake with the valuable and significant objective you expect to accomplish is one technique to help yourself feel more motivated.

In other words, you must use imagery to remind your brain why you are doing this. Imagine how, in the future, working on this spreadsheet will make you richer, more successful in your job, and less anxious this evening. Think about the consequences of not doing it: you'll fall behind in your job and won't be able to reach your objectives.

Imagine what it would be like to have rippling abs and 10% body fat if you're having trouble getting motivated to work out. Now seem worthwhile?

Making whatever you're doing more engaging and enjoyable can increase its salience to your brain, which is a piece of further advice. Making the scene or paragraph, you're writing more engaging is, in my opinion, the greatest treatment for writer's block. It won't be entertaining to read if it isn't interesting enough to write about!

As long as the TV isn't too distracting for you to be able to pay attention to what you're doing, you can make data entering a bit more enjoyable by having it playing in the background on the quiet. Watching individuals play video games on YouTube is an excellent alternative since it lacks a storyline but still entertains.

After you're in the zone, check to ensure nothing will disrupt your focus. Your phone should be quiet.

Power Of Meditation

The practice of meditation is another method. Nothing mysterious about meditation; it's simply about controlling your attention and bringing your thoughts into focus. Meditation trains the mind to become distraction-free and concentrate only on one subject. This method may help you develop tremendous attention and discipline by physically training your salience network, like exercising your muscles in the gym.

Meditation lets you separate from those stressful distractions and let go of anything on your mind.

Everyone should practice meditation since it may potentially boost their well-being, productivity, and attention.

The only issue? If you lack motivation, it might be challenging to start meditation. So, my advice is to begin with brief (5-minute) sessions and attempt to incorporate this into an existing habit that is a part of your daily routine. If you often exercise, consider practicing meditation after your workouts. Or how about adding a little meditation period after brushing your teeth?

And if you find it difficult to stay focused when meditating, think about utilizing a program like Headspace (www.headspace.com) to lead you through it.

Chapter 2
Stop Procrastination

One of your greatest challenges to reaching your goals is procrastination. We wish to do many things but never get around to doing them. This is often due to a lack of focused, intentional effort.

So maybe time is to blame. We could say that we'd love to start our own company, make improvements to our house, publish a book, get in shape, or even clean the kitchen, but we simply don't have the time since we're so busy taking care of our families and working.

Simply said, this is false.

Although 24 hours (16 of which are spent awake) might not seem like much, it should be more than enough to complete everything you want. After all, you watched a whole box set of your preferred TV program only last month.

You didn't finish the most recent Call of Duty game, did you?

Did you not watch TV or browse Facebook for more than an hour? Many nights last week?

Of course, you would have succeeded in your objectives if you had used all that time constructively and productively. And, most likely, a lot more. You may even be fluent in five languages at this very moment!

The issue is exacerbated by procrastination. However, the true cause of this is far more serious energy and discipline problems. You'll discover how to address those issues in this manual.

Why You Lack Discipline

Lack of discipline is the root cause of procrastination. This happens when you sit down to work, and your mind wanders immediately.

This ultimately depends on a few things. To begin with, the task you must do is perhaps a little dull and unfulfilling. You wouldn't likely put off doing the task if it meant playing a fun computer game or devouring a decadent dessert.

Stress and worry are the main causes of the second issue. When we are nervous or stressed, our minds want to concentrate on the cause of that tension, which prevents us from doing what we need to accomplish. Because of this, we often find ourselves surfing the web to pass the time. It's like putting your head in the sand and hoping the issue will disappear.

The irony is that waiting will just make things worse, of course!

Ultimately, this shows that you are not in charge of your thoughts. This is the monkey mind' at its worst, perfectly illustrating how we may feel out of control when deciding where to focus our energies.

That gets us to the second issue, which is energy.

Frequently, we just lack the energy to complete the task at hand.

Perhaps after a long day at work, you're feeling exhausted.

Need to clean the hoes or do some cleanup. You decide to allow yourself five minutes to relax first since you are too exhausted to accomplish it.

It gradually turns into 10 or twenty minutes. Then it's time for bed.

There are instances when our lack of motivation and willpower is so great that we actively put off going to bed. When all we want to do is sleep, we find ourselves watching bad TV or checking Facebook because we can't bear the notion of getting up to clean our teeth.

Additionally, energy is also much to blame for this. You see, maintaining discipline truly takes effort. Whenever we have to decide, choosing the tougher option takes more effort. Because of this, as the day wears on, we also begin to lose our morality.

At this time, our willpower is worn out. Therefore, we often choose the simple path, and other people be darned!

Now that you know everything, you may wonder how to quit putting things off and develop unbreakable willpower.

Why Discipline Is Crucial

Willpower and discipline are essentially two sides of the same coin, so if you want to develop into a more remarkable, strong, and successful version of yourself, you should try to grow this aspect of your life.

In the end, discipline is about controlling your thoughts and behaviors. You must thus learn to free yourself from your emotional shackles.

It doesn't feel good to work all night. Therefore we don't want to do it. We proceed cautiously while contending with our minds at each process stage.

However, a person who practices self-discipline might simply convince oneself that whether they enjoy something or not, they must do it anyhow because it must be done. They focus on a single target or goal while blocking out all other undesirable thoughts and urges.

This is strong material since it enables you to accomplish any work and acquire total control over what you are doing. However, it also fosters consistency between your actions and words. People will remark that you are determined, disciplined, and unaffected by life's worries. You are not easily disturbed by what people say, frantic to please them, or divided between what to do.

This is quite significant. We often make poor judgments that enrage everyone to appease everyone because we want to be liked. We too often allow our emotions to take control of our arguments and discussions, which leads to poor conversational behavior. And often, we sulk about rather than do the necessary tasks, making life worse for us.

The disciplined individual overcomes this and is, in total, the ability to direct their behavior and response. So how do you develop into that individual?

How to Develop Invincible Discipline

How can one develop discipline?

The same way you learn anything else: doing it repeatedly and becoming stronger.

Additionally, this implies that you must be aware of the discipline present at all times. The deliberate decision to ignore distractions and maintain one's attention is discipline. Procrastination is a distraction, and distraction is procrastination. Therefore, you are responsible for paying close attention to what others say while conversing with you.

It is your responsibility to resist the impulse to glance up while you should be working in the office but are curious about what is occurring on the other side of the room. It's your responsibility to push through fatigue while attempting to work out yet feeling exhausted.

Realizing that your sentiments are irrelevant is the first step. It doesn't matter if you're a little hungry, bored, cold, or sleepy as long as you're not harming yourself. It makes no difference whether you believe you deserve a reward. Adulthood is all about overcoming obstacles.

Your desire to concentrate on the things you must concentrate on to achieve your objectives.

This form of 'incidental' training uses your encounters and interactions as opportunities to improve your discipline and attention. But you may also include more training opportunities in your daily schedule.

Use a chilly shower as an example. It takes a great deal of effort and discipline to stand in a cold shower, and your body and mind will constantly battle you while you're doing it. But if you can muster the resolve to plunge into the chilly water, you will be strengthening and developing your willpower. Cold showers are incredibly beneficial since they stimulate blood circulation, help us make more testosterone, and strengthen our immune systems.

Another example is making your bed. If you can successfully convince yourself to make your bed every morning, even when you're anxious or in a hurry, this will be fantastic practice for getting yourself to do other things that you need to. It's a pretty easy habit to get into.

Guys, this is a huge one. Stopping your masturbation is one of the most crucial things you can do to improve your discipline. This is the influence of the 'nofap' movement, which urges men to cease viewing porn and to find fulfillment in sex exclusively.

Porn has the drawback of giving us too much stimulus and too much pleasure too quickly. Our fantastic chemical reward is always "on tap" for us to quickly reach, effectively teaching us to give in to lower cravings. There is no need to wait, no labor to be done, and no need to be disciplined.

The same holds for any other "bad habit" you often indulge in, even if it merely entails thinking unfavorable things. Although it may seem excessive, when you give in to your desires physically or mentally, you are strengthening negative habits and eroding your willpower.

This is why engaging in different types of abstinence may be effective training grounds for developing discipline. I'm not advocating you become a monk; rather, I'm saying that if you're serious about beating procrastination, you need to be able to resist each temptation that comes your way.

The Value of Rewards

I'm not trying to get you to become a monk here. Maintaining discipline and resisting procrastination is necessary, but it's also crucial to have fun. No of what they tell you, nobody will ever get 100% of the time, 100% of the punishment. Being too rigid and restrained might eventually result in more significant problems.

Instead, I advise you to treat yourself to incentives at fixed hours and only once you've earned them. Do you want a large chocolate bar to eat? Indeed, you can. But only after you've managed to stick to your daily calorie limit for the whole day.

Do you want to relax and read an excellent book? It's okay. However, you must first do X amount of labor to have it under your belt.

Can't maintain the nap? OkayOkay, but keep it to once a week at a certain time, and be brief!

Giving yourself incentives for excellent conduct is a terrific approach to boost your motivation and enable you to have fun without fully giving up on being rigorous and disciplined.

Your regular job might be a straightforward illustration of this. It's time to reverse how you typically begin your workday by obtaining a cup of tea and then chatting. You will now get the cup of tea and the conversation as a reward for doing further nice deeds. Those activities are only permitted after you have finished a certain amount of labor. This inspires you and makes it possible for you to work uninterrupted. Put your phone on quiet and permit yourself to check it once per hour for five minutes.

Because you don't have to have a strong enough will to avoid ever performing that activity, doing this helps you avoid procrastinating. It just has to be powerful enough to delay for a while.

One Last Thing...

Finally, you may meditate to help yourself stop putting things off.

In essence, meditation is a discipline-building practice. By applying this technique, you may become far less readily dominated by stress, exhaustion, hunger, or other urges, which involves attempting to block out distracting ideas for only a little time. We become much more disciplined, less stressed, and much better able to concentrate and focus for extended periods of time after practicing meditation.

Of course, it calls for self-control. Build up from there, starting with brief five-minute workouts a few times each week!

Chapter 3
Getting Past Fear

Want to develop into your most amazing, unstoppable self?

I'm not referring to the typical "self-help" material. This goes beyond having a marginally more positive experience with the other sex or being marginally more productive.

Want to improve and change yourself? Want to take on all new challenges?

The solution is to face your fear, then. What is preventing you is your fear. You are becoming less strong and competent because of your fear. And it is your fear that is robbing you of pleasure and fulfillment.

It's time to eradicate fear and realize our entire potential permanently.

Code of the Samurai

We may look to certain historical instances to understand how to overcome fear effectively. The samurai were among the most courageous, powerful warriors ever. How did they accomplish this total absence of fear, then?

Legend has it that the samurai would rehearse a method just before a fight to help them overcome their dread. They would do this by vividly imagining every scenario in which they may die. They would see themselves being beheaded, mutilated, and impaled.
They would next concentrate on embracing these possibilities and adjusting to them. They would accept a horrible, relentless end.

In reality, the samurai were a highly fatalistic and gloomy group. The Bushido code emphasized that dying in combat was an honor and that one should never stop thinking about dying.

Contrary to what you would expect, this gave them greater authority to be the utterly ruthless, fearless warriors they were. This is logical: if you dread death, you'll also fear life.

What cause do the samurai have to be terrified if they have accepted the worst thing that might happen to them and are at peace with it?

Imagine battling someone who has no fear of dying: someone who is prepared to take risks, throw oneself wholeheartedly into a cause, and isn't worried about the possible results. They'd be disastrous.

The good news is that you probably don't need to accept your death in nearly the same manner since you live in a lot less risky period. However, we can use this idea to examine how we may use it.

Taking Notes From The Stoics

Interestingly, stoic philosophers had a similar outlook on their worries. According to the Stoics, the key to happiness is to be ready for any negative consequence and live within those possibilities. They believed being too optimistic was one of the easiest ways to become unpleasant and depressed.

Consider this: if you consistently hope for the worse and get the best, you will either experience a pleasant surprise or receive what you anticipate.

You will repeatedly be let down if you regularly hope for the best and get the worse.

There is no reason not to take chances and risks if you acknowledge that bad things might happen and have planned for them.

And even when things go wrong, there is beauty in it. We have lost things we cared about, which makes the darkest times in our life full of feelings. Living a simple and boring life is the only way to prevent it. Boring daily existence. The times when our biology and psychology were put to the test, and we had to rely on our brains and our fortitude to survive are the occasions when we felt scared for our lives.

The stoics noted that we are most inclined to curse the sky when startled. For example, you don't curse when it begins to rain since this is a common occurrence that we expect. You curse after burning your hand because you were taken aback.

If you anticipate problems, they won't surprise you.

Setting Fear

Tim Ferriss wrote The Four-Hour Workweek. This book is about discovering methods to make your profession fit around your lifestyle rather than the other way around. This entails selecting what you want out of life and then designing a profession around it.

According to Tim, many of us will continue working at jobs we despise and leading unfulfilling lives because we fear the consequences of taking a gamble. Our companions could abandon us if we travel. If we start a new job, we risk failing, becoming bankrupt, and homelessness. We could get a rejection from all angles if we search for a new position.

We cannot go ahead while we are immobilized by fear. We are inherently risk-averse, so we'd prefer to hold on to what little we have instead of moving ahead to claim the great rewards.

To overcome this, Tim organized stoic philosophers' ideas into a method that anybody might apply to overcome their paralyzing anxieties.

The procedure is as follows:

1. Decide what you want to alter or what your aim is first. Let's imagine that you wish to leave your work and start your own company.

2. Next, list the potential negative outcomes and the things you are frightened of. First, your partner can feel that you are careless and decide to break up with you. Second, your new company could not succeed, leaving you with debt. Third, your home can be seized by the bank. Fourth, you could become homeless. Fifth, you could be mocked by your friends.

Sixth, even if everything goes according to plan, you may still detest your new job even more. You see what I mean.

3. Now assign a realistic probability to each of those events. Would your spouse break up with you? We may give it a "2" since it's rare unless there are issues in your marriage to begin with. Would you become homeless, or even if it's a step down from what you previously did, would you probably find another job? That one gets a "3."

4. Do these things matter, then? From 1 to 10, give them a grade. Who cares if your buddies think poorly of you?

5. You will review that list again and jot down how you may deal with unfortunate events. These are the backup plans you have and the coping mechanisms you may use. For instance, if you are in financial difficulty, you might apply for benefits, use some of your savings, ask your parents for assistance, or take on part-time work. You might live out your goal of traveling the globe if your spouse left you.

6. Then go through the list once again. This time, list all the ways to reduce the danger so that it

occurs less often. Concerned about accruing debt? Then create a company plan without a significant up-front cost, and bootstrap your way to success. Do you fear quitting your position? Then launch your company in your spare time.

Now you're going to do something else: you're going to consider the worst-case scenario if your plan isn't carried out.

You can find yourself trapped in a job you detest as a result. That when you're 80 years old, you'll look back on your life and feel as if you accomplished nothing. Your physical and mental health suffered from a lack of exercise or experience.

What is worse? I understand how I feel!

And keep in mind what we spoke about in the stoicism section: unpleasant things will happen. It is impossible to stop all negative things from occurring. You are solely in charge of your feelings at the moment. Don't even attempt always to please everyone since you can't. Your main priorities should be accepting this fact and taking the necessary steps for your emotional and psychological welfare.

Tim also lives by the maxim, "Don't ask for

permission; ask for forgiveness." If traveling or starting a company will make your spouse miserable, then be it. You cannot exist without ever taking a risk because of someone else; else, bitterness would consume you. And you may pass away tomorrow or suffer limb loss in a car accident. Perhaps your lover will leave you for another person!

It's up to them how they respond to your choice. But you can't let it dictate how you behave.

You can't cling to things as they are right now. There is no way to stop horrible things from occurring. All you can do right now is enjoy life to the fullest and the richest. You must thus take those dangers.

Taking a Risk

The method described above may be used when deciding on a major course of action or your future. But what about that strong phobia? That momentary dread?

An identical procedure is used in this case. Fearful of speaking in front of others? Then rapidly go through the fear-inducing exercise, examining the likely consequences and why they are unimportant. Ultimately, you have two options: keep silent and remain afraid, or take risks and develop personally so that you're less afraid the next time.

Consider doing a bungee leap. Alternatively, consider every scenario that may go wrong and how probable or catastrophic it is. The possibility that the rope may break or be too lengthy exists, but you know that the chance of that occurring is very low—probably about 0.0001% or less.

Additionally, it would end immediately, and you wouldn't remember a thing.

You also cannot live in constant terror. So leap!

A proverb goes that you cannot control what occurs to you, but you can control how you respond to it. Let's go back to the stoics for a second. Remember this and maintain your composure even when everything around you is collapsing.

A little CBT, mindfulness training and meditation may assist with this. The term "cognitive behavioral therapy" (CBT) is a psychotherapy intervention that advocates altering thinking processes to alter feelings and behaviors. One effective technique is "thought challenging," simply fear setting. Here, you only examine your limiting ideas and beliefs and determine their viability or reality. Sounds recognizable?

Unsurprisingly, CBT is one of the most popular techniques for overcoming phobias.

But 'hypothesis testing' is a concept from CBT that is much more effective. This implies that you put your ideas to the test in the real world rather than merely in your head.

If you have a paralyzing fear of public speaking, you could purposely deliver a bad speech when you take the stage. By going through it, you verify that the 'worst case scenario' isn't all that horrible.

By practicing this, you may develop a desensitization to the things that might otherwise scare you and grow into a lot more fearless and self-assured version of yourself.

And the greatest approach to conquering fear is continually pushing yourself and taking on new challenges. Continue putting yourself through the exact challenges you find difficult. The more you practice keeping your thoughts calm and steady in these circumstances, the more you'll discover that reacting comes easily. Fear is a positive indication since it shows that you're maturing.

One additional thing: don't forget to breathe! A deep breath will engage your parasympathetic nervous system, which will cause your heart rate to decrease and your fear reaction to be lessened.

Keep your sights on the end goal: if you can finally conquer your fear, you can overcome any obstacle.

Chapter 4
Improved Self-Confidence

Increasing your self-confidence is one of the finest things you can do if you want to enhance every aspect of your life. When you have low self-esteem, everything you do will be less pleasurable since you'll always feel horrible about yourself.

However, you will 'give off' low self-esteem to other people. Whether you want it to or not, this emanates from you, which may reduce your influence on others. Searching for a promotion? Your employers will learn from your low self-esteem that you are unsure of your ability to do the necessary tasks, and they will be less inclined to trust you with more responsibility.

Want to have a successful love life? A strong warning indication that you are not a good catch is having low self-esteem. Why would the other person believe you are a good catch when you do not think you are?

This could ultimately result in a prediction coming true. People will regard you like you're useless if you behave worthless and don't take risks, and you won't be able to succeed.

Look for chances. As a result, you will fall further behind your peers, lowering your self-esteem.

So how can you escape this situation? What is the solution?

In this article, we'll look at how you may increase your self-assurance and develop into the strong alpha male or assertive wonder woman you have the potential to be.

Why Developing Self-Confidence Will Change Your Life

Let's first examine why self-confidence is so crucial and how it may fundamentally alter everything.

Do you remember when you were younger and had feelings for the student at your school? Your mother responded when you informed her that confidence is key.

You probably believed this was a deception and all about money or appearances. Car bumper stickers advise you to "just be yourself" and that it's "all about confidence." It's a great platitude, but in the end, it's simply a fiction to boost our self-esteem. Right?

Wrong!

All of it comes down to having self-confidence. I know a few men who are neither affluent nor physically fit, nor are they handsome in the traditional sense. Nevertheless, they attract a lot of females, and the reason is obvious: they are gregarious and entertaining.

For this reason, the 'bad dudes' are known for getting all the chicks. These men act however they choose and don't care what others think. This has a confident air about it and looks quite well.

Women experience the same thing. If she knows how to flirt (which comes from confidence!) and dresses to impress (which comes from confidence!), a woman who is a 6 out of 10 can defeat an 8 out of 10.

There is a catch: no amount of confidence can help you if you lack social skills. You also need to improve on it, as you'll discover below. Otherwise, confidence is everything.

The same holds for your work and how you fit in with your buddies.

Everyone has met someone who exudes extreme confidence and is gorgeous and accomplished. We all want to be just like them.

And the reason for this is that confidence communicates that you are in a position of authority over others. We want to date individuals who, in the dating game, we consider "out of our league." From a biological point of view, this is the greatest method to guarantee that our DNA flourishes and it also helps us feel good about ourselves.

We may infer from someone's confidence that they must be an evolutionary catch. We are attracted to them unconsciously because we believe it would elevate our status. However, someone who has little regard for himself will be disregarded and used in the meantime.

Although it seems harsh, this is regrettably simply human nature.

How to Increase Confidence

How, then, should you go about gaining that confidence boost?

There are two distinct directions to go in: internal and outward. Although it is far simpler to develop external confidence, internal confidence will alter who you are and how you feel about yourself.

Starting with the simpler, shallower solution, we'll next go on to the more significant adjustment we can make.

Shallow Confidence Boost

Change what you can about yourself to better match yourself with what you believe a successful person should be since this will help you feel more confident right away. For instance, most believe successful individuals are more beautiful and intelligent. We could feel uneasy about ourselves because we dislike our appearance.

Correcting it is the first and easiest step.

Making a significant adjustment is one of the finest methods to alter how we feel about our appearance. Although it may seem like a corny technique to increase our self-confidence, getting a makeover works.

Here, it's important to be courageous and modify aspects of yourself that you would otherwise be reluctant to do. You want to make adjustments that people will truly notice so that people will pay attention to you when you enter a place. You want to feel like a new person and want other people to think of you differently than they did previously.

Therefore, for ladies, sporting bright red lipstick, higher heels, or a lower-cut top may all be beneficial, particularly if these are things that you ordinarily wouldn't do.

For men, this may include donning a suit jacket, obtaining a significantly shorter hairstyle, or donning a tank top to display your arms.

Most individuals can name a few things they would be afraid to wear but know look excellent on self-assured, beautiful people. What's this?

Confidence is the only thing lacking, even if you are gorgeous. If you wear that attire, you'll seem that confident, greatly increasing your confidence.

You should still be who you are, of course. Wearing items that you don't enjoy or that make you feel unauthentic is not advised.

But just try to get outside your comfort zone and potentially surprise others. Likewise, spend some time on your appearance, clothing, and grooming. Spend a bit extra money on textiles of higher quality, and spend some time moisturizing and doing your hair. Demonstrating that you believe you are "worth it" also sends out strong signals.

If this is too much for you, think about hiring a stylist! Some professionals do this for a livelihood and can make you feel fantastic. Women, you may want to take a cosmetics lesson!

Enjoy the looks you get when you enter the workplace now. Work on your appearance.

Internal Positivity

This last confidence-boosting example works because it starts a "virtuous cycle." One positive development will inevitably lead to another in other works. You'll wear more assured clothing, making other individuals behave differently toward you. As a result, you will become

Feel more certain, and you'll begin to project greater assurance.

But to improve your self-assurance, you'll need to put more effort into cultivating your inner sense of satisfaction.

And you are aware of the origin of this?

Quit worrying about what others may think.

What confidence actually is is this. The individual who spreads out in a fashion that makes them feel comfortable no matter what other people think, rather than one done to make them "look more impressive," is the most confident person in the room.
The individual who isn't scared to offend someone with what they say is the one who actually impresses. They are not about to concur with the majority opinion only to gain favor. They express their opinions while, of course, maintaining politeness toward others.

So how do you go at this point? When did you stop worrying about what other people thought?

The solution is to be aware of who you are and what matters to you. Find your life's "goal," your genuine purpose, and what you want to achieve by taking some time to ponder.

Once you have accomplished this, you can begin working toward your objective and directing your attention toward the important things to you. And after you've accomplished that, you can ignore criticism or other people's views.

Are people making fun of your height? When being a great writer is your objective, what does it matter? Uncertain as to whether a group will like you? When you know your genuine pals, what difference does it make?

You will become resistant to other people's judgments when you know and evaluate yourself according to your standards, which will also enable you to fortify your resolve and determination.

And as a result, you will become a lot more captivating and fascinating. Speaking from a place of passion and not caring as much about what others think of you will make you seem a lot more mysterious and fascinating. If you don't attempt to satisfy everyone around you, others will eventually try to please you.

And this is the path to absolute, unflinching certainty.

Develop Your Confidence

This assurance won't come overnight, just like anything else. It must be trained in addition to being practiced. And it operates according to the SAID principle, just as training for any other activity would. 'Specific Adaptations to Imposed Demands' is the abbreviation for this phrase. In other words, we become better at whatever we do often. You must challenge yourself to do things that you would typically find intimidating and repeatedly reinforce your good sentiments if you want to gain greater confidence and stop caring about what other people think.

This will be the ideal opportunity to exercise your new self-worth if, for example, you are often too timid and insecure to speak in front of others. Make an effort to speak out in front of others. Better push yourself to make mistakes on purpose to develop your ability to accept responsibility. The worst that can happen is that you befuddle a stranger, so remind yourself that it doesn't matter what these people think. What happens doesn't matter, so practice introducing yourself to people and initiating conversations. All that counts is that you are molding yourself into the person you want to be. You may even consider enrolling in a stand-up.

For instance, taking a comedy or theatre class might help remove inhibitions.

You may learn to respond correctly to the remarks and responses of others and learn to concentrate more on what is really important to you with the aid of meditation and CBT (cognitive behavioral therapy).

You'll discover that you gradually become like yourself if you can accomplish it. You are prospering due to living up to the standards you have set for yourself.

You need to quit thinking about what other people may say and instead concentrate on how it makes you feel to wear that bolder and more colorful approach.
And as soon as you start to feel this kind of confidence, you'll see that it builds up steadily until it becomes large. Others will support every action you take, and each victory will boost your confidence and enable you to concentrate on new tasks.

Chapter 5
A Healthier You

One of the most crucial areas to start if you want to improve who you are and start a transition that will affect all elements of your life is your health.

Your strength comes from your whole wellness. The amount of work you can do that day will depend on how you feel when you get up in the morning. Your emotions, your capacity to execute cognitively or physically taxing activities, and even how you appear are all directly impacted by your health. The length and quality of your life will depend on how well you can maintain your health.

In other words, your health is crucial if you want to improve your life objectively. Nevertheless, many of us don't give it much consideration.

Most of us place much more importance on our employment, how neat the home is, and what our friends think of us than on our physical fitness, heart health, or how much body fat we carry.

So it should not be surprising that many of us are in really poor health. Many of us go to work by car each day, where we then spend the whole day slumped over in an office, feeling very agitated. When we go home, we eat.

We eat a prepared dinner devoid of nutrition and high in salt and sugar, after which we flop on the sofa and sleep fitfully for an all-too-short time.

Then we ponder why we are unhealthy, ugly, exhausted, down, and sad.

Hmm!

The main issue is that many of us are unaware of how to address this issue and improve our health. Furthermore, many of us believe that achieving health will take a lot of labor and effort, which is too much for us to do.

Maybe you've tried a new diet or exercise regimen in the past and discovered that it didn't provide the outcomes you were hoping for. Or maybe you gave it a go and ran out of energy initially?

Let's investigate our options in that regard.

How to Approach Food

Since changing one's diet is ultimately the easiest thing to do, we'll start there.

Our first goal is to improve your health since doing so will make losing weight and becoming in shape simpler. So don't concentrate on depriving yourself.
Even if it causes weight reduction, that isn't 'healthy'.

Understanding that food is more than "fuel" requires a significant mental change. Many of us approach our diets similarly to how we may approach the petrol we put in our cars. We notice that we need to refuel when we become hungry and exhausted. Therefore, we look for whatever kind of food we can, ideally something good, and then we eat till we are satisfied.

Food is not only fuel, however. The fact that food is both a resource and a substance is more significant than the fact that it serves as fuel. The body is composed of this. Our bodies recycle the nutrients from our foods into the building blocks for our bones, muscles, and brains. As a result, vital hormones and neurotransmitters are produced, enabling a wide range of bodily responses and functions. And we use it in the battle against sickness and cancer.

If all you consider is "filling yourself up," your body

won't get the essential nutrients it needs, so you'll start feeling bloated.

Sluggish and exhausted. At that point, you start to see signs of aging, such as skin peeling, bloodshot eyes, and brittle hair.

Did you know, for example, that 80% of Americans are magnesium deficient? Considering all this mineral accomplishes—including preventing muscle pain and aches, accelerating learning through brain plasticity, improving sleep, and aiding men in producing more testosterone for increased virility and masculinity, it is a staggering number that is devastating.

This one vitamin alone does all of those things. Imagine what would happen if there weren't enough.
Then there is vitamin D, which we may get from food or the sun. Once again, a large portion of us is deficient due to our desk-bound indoor lives, which include reduced testosterone production, poor sleep, depressed mood, and increased vulnerability to disease. Vitamin D functions as a "master key" for many of your hormones and, among other things, aids in controlling your appetite and energy levels.

According to studies, consuming more vitamin D may help people avoid major illnesses, saving thousands of lives every year!

Following that is vitamin B12. This vitamin improves the body's production and use of red blood cells, allowing us to carry nutrients and energy to our muscles and brain. This is low in many individuals, particularly vegetarians, which may lead to inflammation, depression, and nerve damage.

I could continue forever. Most of us don't consume enough essential fatty acids, vitamins, amino acids, minerals, or other essential nutrients, all performing vital and significant bodily tasks. We consume empty calories from processed sweet meals like cake, sausage rolls, and Coca-Cola.

I thus want you to accomplish the following three things:

1. Change to natural, fresh meals. That implies that you should try to consume meals prepared yourself from scratch at least four times every week. It doesn't have to be difficult or costly to achieve this. It may be as simple as ordering some chicken with some broccoli and rice or ordering a salad with tuna, tomatoes, avocado, and other healthy ingredients. This is not more costly than a prepackaged meal and just takes a few minutes to prepare.

2. Consume a multivitamin. Although getting the

nutrients we need through our food is preferable, many of us will fall short of this goal, leaving us with little choice except to obtain them via supplements. Nothing is wrong with carrying this out. Increasing your levels of those important nutrients doesn't harm you as long as it absorbs them.

3. Look for nutrient-dense meals and superfoods. For instance, you sometimes need to drink smoothies. I suggest trading your morning coffee for a fruit smoothie on the way to work (or, even better, a veggie smoothie with less sugar). Similarly, I advise cooking many eggs to be eaten as snacks over the next week. These are comprehensive supplies of the necessary amino acids and are rich in the brain-boosting 'choline'. Avocados are fantastic because they include magnesium, good saturated fats, and other nutrients.

Finally, if you want to supplement your diet further, here are some items you may include to feel and function much better:

- **Lutein:** Previously praised mainly for its advantages for the eyes, lutein is a vitamin that may boost mental acuity and energy levels.

- **Magnesium Threonate:** will improve your sleep and fortify your brain when taken before bed.

- **Omega 3 fatty acid** fights brain fog and joint discomfort by reducing inflammation and protecting cells from harm. It accelerates cell communication to improve brain function.

- **Cordyceps:** Cordyceps may help you recover from chronic stress and adrenal exhaustion. By using supplements to combat one of our current health problems, you may boost your energy levels and avoid exhaustion-related illnesses.

The idea is that by making these adjustments, you ought to begin to feel and look better. Your brain will function more quickly, you'll feel better, and you'll have more energy. As a result, it will be simpler for you to start concentrating on other parts of your health, such as exercise and weight reduction.

Fixing Your Fitness

Aiming too high is a mistake most individuals make while attempting to improve their health and fitness. When they can now hardly make it up the stairs, their goal is often to attempt to change their bodies into the athletic specimens they see on magazine covers.

Running makes this very clear. Many individuals stop running because they dislike it so much. They find it awful because they exert too much effort, run too quickly, and go too far in their pursuit of fame as elite runners or the burning of many calories.

However, the ideal strategy for running is to initially just concentrate on becoming better at it. Even better, you ought to develop a liking for jogging.

You should start with shorter runs and move more slowly to accomplish this. Go for a casual jog in a beautiful region, and as soon as you become tired of it, return home. If you do this often enough, you'll gradually begin to like and anticipate such runs. At this point, they may start to change their lifestyle and fitness.

You may train your heart by running only once or twice a week. Never undervalue the impact this may have on your well-being and happiness. Running especially will help to strengthen and expand the left ventricle. Your heart will ultimately be able to pump more blood throughout the body with fewer beats. Therefore, your vital "resting heart rate" statistic will slow down. As you exercise, your heart will beat less quickly, improving your sympathetic tone. In other words, you will have far less constant stress and cardiac pressure.

However, you could not be a runner. You may not be able to do this. Then you should start doing resistance training, sometimes known as weight lifting.

Weightlifting can change your life, and this is a fact. More individuals ought to think about it.

Many women, as well as many males, will shy away. Since they don't want to become extremely muscular or bulky, they shy away from the thought of weight lifting. These individuals overlook that it is impossible to 'accidentally' develop excessive muscle mass. The size of Arnold Schwarzenegger was not acquired by chance. Instead, you need intense training and effort to get that size.

A more moderate exercise regimen will give you muscle tone, power, and better body control. And what's this? Simply having muscle will raise your metabolism to the point where it will help you lose weight.

So even when you sleep, you'll be burning extra calories. Oh, and it also provides you with the desired optimum proportions.

PPL - Push Pull Legs is a fantastic workout program for beginners to attempt. Consequently, you train all pushing motions one day, all pulling movements the next, and legs on the third day. Once again, don't exert too much pressure too soon. Just enjoy the workout and try new things with your body.

There is no haste since you are not an athlete. There is no need to exert more effort than you find entertaining.

Finally, remember that you should also be more active during the day. Two or three one-hour weekly sessions cannot compensate for a sedentary lifestyle. Start incorporating walking into your routine to burn an extra 1,000–1,500 calories every workweek—an additional 200–300 calories daily!

Likewise, consider enrolling in a class, whether it's dancing, martial arts, or any physically active activity that can help you lose weight.

Chapter 6
How to Form Effective Habits

Humans are habitual beings. Through thousands of years of evolution, we have developed a preference for regularity, predictability, and a predetermined sequence of events.

Therefore, most of us have a daily schedule that we stick to. Maybe you wake up, make breakfast, shower, put on clothes, and watch the news with a cup of coffee for ten minutes before rushing to the bus.

You probably follow a similar nightly pattern that includes a 10-minute trip to the grocery store, cooking supper, watching TV, showering, and then reading a book in bed. Most likely, you go to bed at the same hour every day.

There is no chance of this. It all boils down to how our brains are wired. How our biology functions and how our minds function.

The fact that we continuously use the same neural pathways and set off the same connections indicates that we are effectively repeating the same actions or ideas. These connections are myelinated as a result of what we do.

That indicates that myelin sheaths act as insulation, making them stronger and stronger. One activity will become so entrenched as to become automatic and out of our conscious control if we repeat it enough times after another.

Ivan Pavlov, a psychologist, did an excellent job demonstrating this when he trained dogs to salivate when they heard a bell.

This is also why people with significant brain injury who cannot recall their names may be able to perform magnificent piano concertos. Some people can play the piano without even being aware of it! The motor neurons are simply hardwired as a result of years of experience. To make a lasting impression, the groove has been repeatedly oiled.

Our biology, on the other hand, is fully reliant on rhythms and patterns. Nitric oxide and cortisol are released when the sun rises at a certain moment. These neurotransmitters set off a chain reaction in the brain, increasing alertness and activity. After eating, we calmed down a little more and prepared for work.

Due to a melatonin and serotonin boost, we slow down and become more lethargic around 4 p.m. By the time the sun sets. We are creating more melatonin and finding it more and more difficult to think as adenosine builds up in our brains.

This may throw your whole schedule out of sync and make you feel out of sorts if you get up at a different time, the sun rises at a different time, or you eat a larger meal. This causes jet lag, and changing your mealtimes is one way to combat it.

In other words, the more often we repeat a behavior, the more difficult it is to modify that pattern.

This is terrible news if the conduct in issue includes smoking. However, it's fantastic news if the habit includes going to the gym. Since the age of 13 (I will be 30 this year), I have exercised at least four days a week. I've been regularly doing something for 17 years. You may assume that I now find it quite difficult to stop. Going to the gym is effortless for me since I like working out, and it's a big part of who I am.

In other words, using the force of habit to your advantage may help you achieve any goal in life, whether it be financial, either a better physique or a wealthier financial account.

How do you go about developing such habits?

How to Form New Behaviors

The Thirty-Day Rule

You will often read that repeating activity for thirty days is the greatest method to establish a new habit. If you succeed in doing that, you will have sufficiently engrained the habit that you won't be able to quit.

Is this a fact? Theoretically, thirty days would be sufficient for you to practice an activity sufficiently for it to become at least partly entrenched, but that "magic number" is quite arbitrary. There is no justification for why completing a task in thirty days should be superior to doing it in 29 or 31 days.

Anecdotal evidence is what this theory has going for; the study indicates that it seems correct, and if you can maintain a new habit for that long, you'll at least be on the right road.

This also makes leaving a bit simpler. Exercise first thing in the morning might be more bearable if you know you just have to do it for 30 days rather than believing you always do it.

Little Behaviors

Do you find it difficult to floss your teeth every day for the next 30 days? If so, you may want to consider employing something known as "micro habits." A micro habit is simply a means to cheat the 30-day trial by figuring out how to continue your habit for that long without effort and then extrapolating the benefits.

Simply put, a micro habit breaks down your new desired behavior into something basic and easy to keep. So, for instance, your new objective can be to floss one tooth and do so every night. Sticking to this task shouldn't be tough since it takes two seconds.

However, just as with a "full-sized" habit, you should discover that this micro habit becomes deeply embedded after some time, and you finally find it simple to keep to it. All that's left to do is grow this practice until you're flossing every tooth!

If you intended to create a book, you might set a goal of writing only one line every night as a more practical version of this. Similar to how you may strive to do 20 press-ups every day to become in shape.

This works best when what you're doing still has value on its own. Even if you performed 20 press-ups, you would still see some results.

For instance, improvement. Likewise, a book might still be written if one phrase was read each night. Avoid a situation where you could consider your micro habit "pointless" and disregard it.

The amazing thing about micro habits is that you will discover that occasionally you wind up doing more right from the start. The toughest part is usually simply starting, so if you aim to do 20 press-ups, you'll probably perform a whole exercise nonetheless.

The fact that you may choose to default to the micro habit is what's crucial, however. It matters more that you continue to include something in your routine than the habit itself (for the time being!).

Context

Try associating your new habit with your current routine and environment to develop new habits.

In other words, adding flossing to your existing routine, like cleaning your teeth, is a good idea if you want to develop the habit.

Pick a certain time of day to iron your shirts after, such as preparing your morning tea, if you want to develop the habit of doing so.

This works because it links your brain's previous behaviors to your new ones. Every time you brew your morning tea, a network of neurons in your body ignites. Those neurons should light up the new network for ironing clothing when they fire. They are interrelated.

This is also true practically: you must choose an appropriate moment for the initiation of your new habit as well as an appropriate setting for it. And you should know that the specified time and location will always be convenient. You must always be able to exercise here, at this time.

For instance, I had previously planned to include daily meditation in my practice. Since there always appeared to be more essential things to accomplish and I could never find the appropriate moment, I first struggled. I, therefore, combined my meditation and exercise sessions. I just said I would meditate for 5 (yes, 5!) minutes right after a workout since I already worked out 4-5 times a week. I'd always be in the proper spot to exercise that micro habit—the gym—and it wouldn't take up much time.

Maintaining consistency in your surroundings and environment is crucial since everything around you might reinforce your habit. This is why it's usually advised to modify your environment immediately while attempting to stop a habit. One of the first things you're advised to do if you're attempting to quit anything, like alcohol or drugs, is to stop hanging out with the same individuals in the exact locations. These are now 'triggers' since they have come to be linked to the habit.

Triggers are beneficial, however, if the habit is a good one.

The Power of Habit

A single action is a habit, but you have a routine when combining many actions.

I previously discussed the usefulness of forming routines and planning where you will be and what time you will accomplish something. This is crucial for reaching objectives, and if you can create a routine for yourself that includes a variety of positive habits, you'll find that your chances of success across the board are much increased.

For instance, if you're starting a new training program, you must know exactly when and where you'll work out. Additionally, you must 'hang' this new habit from your routine and behaviors.

It is insufficient to merely state that you will exercise "five days a week" since you will forget, procrastinate, or feel too exhausted.

Find a place in your schedule where you can always make room instead. The greatest time for me to train is just after I drive my wife to the train station. I go to the gym directly next door and do this every morning. I just have to stroll in my gym gear and work out before I drive home!

There is nothing more since I'm already on the road. The amount of time the trip took. Additionally, I don't do additional washing (which also takes time) until I return home.

Similarly, deciding when to prepare food and how to consume it is necessary to maintain a healthy diet. I achieved this by locating a nearby salad bar that I could visit during my lunch break. I was certain it would always be available, affordable, and reliable.

The best method to achieve your objectives is to establish a routine.

But keep in mind that variety and attempting new things are what give life its worth. Refrain from going backward so you don't atrophy and cease developing. Habits aid in achieving.

Enjoy the scenery while you go, but don't forget to get where you're going.

Chapter 7
Creating a Meaningful Life

What gives life purpose?

Of course, the query is a ruse. There is no right way to conduct your life; everyone will respond differently. Any response would be legitimate, and how you decide to navigate the world is entirely up to you.

However, there are undoubtedly certain things that are meaningless in life. And you may undoubtedly do certain actions to aid in your search for purpose. This article examines how to find meaning in your life and why doing so is so potent and crucial.

Is Life Meaningful for You?

Looking at our current lives can be a good place to start. Where do you now get the meaning from?

There's a chance you'll choose some of the following responses:

- Career

- Family
- Friends
- Partner
- Children
- Travel

Few people would say that "food" or "computer games" are what makes life meaningful. Our travel becomes more significant when our professions and relationships become more important.

The 'Hierarchy of Needs' idea put forward by Maslow is generally supported by this. Maslow was a psychologist who proposed a hierarchy of needs with the most significant requirements at the top and the most urgent needs at the bottom.

Our immediate, basic requirements include things like food, air, and maybe sex, but as we get closer to the top, things become more abstract and inspirational.

His pyramid resembles the image below, from bottom to top:

- Biological requirements: food, air, water, and sex
- Protection from harm, refuge, and predators and aggressors

- Love/belonging: spouse, family, friends, community
- Esteem is a sense of confidence, acceptability, and value.

Personal Development

Thus, the first unexpected finding from this list is that love and belonging are not at the top but somewhere in the center. It seems as if Maslow is trying to convince us that love isn't the source of meaning in life.

Though poets and songwriters may disagree, this is true. Ultimately, you can't get your feeling of fulfillment, purpose, and pleasure just from other people.

First of all, your relationships will suffer as a result of this. You may develop toxic behaviors in that connection, such as being possessive, jealous, clinging, or other negative traits, if you get your meaning from another person and depend on them for your self-worth.

This also makes you very susceptible. Your whole universe will crumble if the source of your meaning changes, and they have to go.

Some individuals have wonderful, ideal families yet lack a feeling of direction or purpose. They are miserable and in a rut because they lack a sense of direction.

Many of us must cope with this since it is so often. This is essentially where the midlife crisis originates!

We have regard farther up the ladder. That is to say, you must learn how to live with yourself, like yourself, to be happy and satisfied, and for life to have a purpose. If not, you will be dissatisfied with all you have accomplished and lack the resources to advance.

But it's still not the top spot. What exactly is self-actualization, then?

The Monomyth

Looking at the monomyth might help us understand what self-actualization can entail. The monomyth, commonly known as the "hero's journey," is a common tale that has been recounted again throughout history and across society. The tales we tell in novels, movies, and comic books are diverse, yet they all eventually convey the same message.

The same hero is taking the voyage.

What exactly is this journey? The story opens with the protagonist in their "regular world." Here, we see them conversing as normal with their family and friends, and we look at them. A call to action follows. This often results from the hero's want to travel and discover. An additional trigger is a provoking event, though, such as the princess being taken or a parent passing away.

The voyage then starts with the hero exploring uncharted territory. 'Crossing the threshold' is the phrase used to describe this. The hero will run across new foes, friends, and threats.

They will eventually arrive at the 'inmost cave,' the most hazardous region of the new world, or the guts of the beast.

The experience follows. The final battle pits the hero against an unbeatable adversary, and they often lose.

Apotheosis follows. The most significant portion of the story occurs here when the protagonist often experiences some kind of metamorphosis and becomes 'divine. They could ascend and become a super saiyan or rise from the grave. In each case, the hero has changed and grown to be more powerful and larger than before.

They engage the adversary, defeat them, and then return home with their love, the elixir, or peace.

This story has been recounted several times. Sometimes, like in movies like The Lord of the Rings or Star Wars, the plot is quite literal. Sometimes the narrative is considerably more psychological or symbolic. In a romantic comedy, the protagonist is often unsatisfied with their lack of love. Crossing the threshold frequently includes choosing to pursue a lady, make friends, or attempt to be "just casual," the apotheosis is typically an epiphany when the protagonist realizes their lack of love.

Acknowledging their mistakes, their love has been there for them the whole time.

The apotheosis, the transformation, and the resurrection are, in any case, the most crucial aspects of this tale and, by extension, of all stories. This is the character arc, giving the whole trip its purpose.

The voyage served just as practice for shaping the person.

Why, therefore, do we react to this so positively? Because it is our tale, that's why. We are all that hero, after all. We all leave the relative safety of our parent's homes to embark on a new profession or enroll in college. By doing this, we develop, change, and adapt. This assists us in getting the career we desire, getting married, and starting a family. Story over. The most significant aspect was our development, challenge, and progress in achieving that objective.

This is also a legacy of our evolutionary past. In the wild, we would have started as a group and gone out independently to seek additional food, shelter, and resources to form our tribe. We would encounter difficulties along the road (snakes!), and consequently, we would become stronger and more intelligent.

This narrative is about development, adventure, and challenge—these things propel us forward as people and species. We won't achieve anything if we remain at ease.

The Evaluation Shadow

The frightening phase is about to start.

Why do so many of us ultimately end up in dead-end positions and feel fairly disappointed as a consequence since it is so firmly instilled into us that we must pursue the things we desire in life, continuously taking on new challenges, and go outside of our comfort zone to become someone new?

This could be explained by a concept known as the evolutionary shadow.

Recall how evolution works. All that matters is surviving. The individual who survives passes on their characteristics, which are probably good characteristics as they enable them to survive. Therefore, all of our DNA is composed of prior "winners," and our mind is tuned to support our survival and well-being.

The issue is that evolution doesn't care about humans beyond age 30—maybe even after age 35.

Why? Because by the time you reach that age, you've either already had children or are in a circumstance where you are ready to have children.

You've played your part and passed on your genes that survived. It thus makes no difference what happens to you after that.

And this may be observed in how we conduct our daily lives. The exploration, discovery, novelty, and adventure are all gone from our life after we get a secure job and have a family. When we become stuck, we begin to go backward rather than ahead.

This is also reflected in the movies, which explains why so few tales about married couples exist. There are very few tales about princes who have already attained the throne and are now responsible for royal administration.

And this is why it seems like our lives sometimes have no purpose. It's a result of their lack of focus.

Apotheosis is actualization. Realization is expansion. We are improving to the best of our abilities.

What a man can be, he must be is a famous quotation often used to explain actualization. You are regressing if you are not realizing your potential or working toward becoming a better version of yourself.

When we challenge the brain, learn something new, and give it a goal, the brain springs to life. As it generates more dopamine, norepinephrine, and BDNF (brain-derived neurotrophic factor), it becomes younger and more plastic. We become more energized and optimistic, and our memory and attention also improve.

But as soon as you quit, your chance of beginning to develop Alzheimer's and other types of cognitive impairment increases significantly. The only thing you can control about your body is whether it travels forward or backward.

How to Find Meaning in Your Life

What is the best way to put all of this theory into practice? What must you truly accomplish to give your life purpose?

The first step in the solution is realizing that a happy family and a successful career are insufficient. Yes, it is crucial to your pleasure, but it doesn't foster change or provide challenges.

You must assume the role of the hero once again to give life purpose. You must undertake that adventure and confront fresh obstacles.

This might imply that you have grand plans for your career, such as being a successful businessperson, top lawyer, or rock musician.

Or it may imply that you engage in a fulfilling activity. You may write a book or learn how to code and create an application.

Consider taking up philosophy to resolve some of life's most important issues.

It may also have to do with charity or family. You can choose to adopt a kid or decide to give back to your community.

You may wish to investigate how your religion contributes to your sense of purpose. Perhaps you wish to travel and explore the globe.

However, there must be a trip and a difficulty involved. Even if the final goal appears unattainable, it must drive you to advance and provide you with a direction. You must be working hard, learning, developing, and enthusiastic about something.

Because life has significance when it has a purpose.

It might be tempting to give in to the lower levels of Maslow's hierarchy: to overindulge in delicious food and stay warm, cozy, and slouchy. That won't, however, fulfill your soul, just your body. Life will gradually lose its color and significance as you rot and disintegrate.

When you are tired, worn down, challenged, and beaten yet you still decide to keep going—that is when you will feel the most alive. When you conquer mountains, you'll feel the most alive. Leave your cozy recliner, enter the deepest cave, and emerge stronger than ever.

Chapter 8
Control Your Mind

An instruction manual of some kind would almost certainly be included if you were to purchase a vehicle, computer, gaming system, or other kinds of toy so that you could learn how to use it.

This is crucial since it enables you to maximize its benefits and prevents errors that can endanger it.

Unfortunately, there is no instruction manual for the world's most significant and complicated things. Consider children as an example. Any new parent will tell you how shocked they were to learn that no one could teach them how to be a good parent.

The biggest one is our own minds, which comes next. These are the most sophisticated supercomputers, and they are responsible for all of our irrational thoughts, emotions, and experiences. However, our brains are left to our devices; they do not arrive with manuals or instructions.

How do you learn to control your brain, then?

Fortunately, researchers studying the brain learn new things about it daily. Although there is still a great deal to learn, we are more knowledgeable than ever before, and we can use this knowledge to improve our happiness, intelligence, and effectiveness. Continue reading to learn how to fully and completely manage your mind.

How the Brain Functions

As I stated, learning neuroscience may take decades, and even then, it will be required to focus on a single field since it is a sophisticated machine. There is much more to it than can be covered in this article, but we can still provide a concise summary to help you understand the fundamental principles of brain function.

What do we know, then?

Neurons are the basic building blocks of the brain. These are neurons, which are cells with lengthy axons and dendrites. These are so close to one another that they practically touch, indicating they are close enough for little signals to pass between them. This leads to a massive map of billions of neurons connected in complex ways. Everybody has a unique connectome, which is a kind of network. Our unique skills, talents, and personalities result from these individual variances.

One or more of these neurons may be linked to each event you have. Each neuron represents perception, memory, experience, emotion, or other concepts. Similar to how your memory comprises interconnected neurons that reflect your thoughts and ideas, your eyesight is mapped to a vast array of neurons representing what you see.

These neurons are loosely divided into several brain areas based on their functions. For instance, the neurons in charge of human vision are entirely located in the occipital lobe. Neurons in the motor cortex relate to all of our body's motions and feelings. In our prefrontal cortex, we manage tasks like motivation and planning.

The brain stem controls breathing in us. And many of our memories are kept in our hippocampus. This is why harm to a particular part of the brain may cause a loss of a certain function, and this structure of the brain is so severe that there have even been instances when a head injury has only caused a patient to lose their memory of veggies.

'Action potentials' are what allow neurons to communicate with one another. These are electrical impulses that appear after a neuron has been stimulated enough. That stimulation often occurs when many adjacent neurons fire vigorously enough to push them over a certain excitability threshold. Neurotransmitters may also be released as a consequence of an action potential. These substances, which are secreted from sacs (cysts), change how

Neurons function, perhaps increasing or decreasing their likelihood to fire or altering how significant, joyful, sad, or remembered an experience seems.

Our hormonal and neurotransmitter balance is another aspect that affects our uniqueness. You will often be in a pleasant and calm mood if you have a lot of the feel-good chemical serotonin. You will be more wired and anxious if you have high levels of cortisol and glutamate.

Outside Factors and Neurotransmitters

Here, it's crucial to understand that those neurotransmitters may also originate from biological signals coming from our bodies, in addition to being a consequence of what is happening in the brain. For instance, when your blood sugar is low, your brain creates more cortisol, a stress hormone. This is an evolutionary reaction designed to help us look for more food, but it is also why we often feel agitated and irritated after not eating for a time. This is the source of the feeling of being "hangry"!

On the other hand, when we consume food and our blood sugar rises, serotonin might be produced. This explains why we feel happy after eating. But gradually, the serotonin transforms into melatonin, the neurotransmitter associated with sleep.

Blocks neuronal activity. This explains why we often feel exhausted and weary after a substantial meal.

Numerous additional factors also affect the equilibrium of our brain neurotransmitters. For example, bright light may wake us up by increasing the synthesis of cortisol and nitric oxide while decreasing the creation of melatonin. Remember that because there were no artificial lights in the environment, our brain could only depend on this signal to determine the time of day.

While there is much more to it than that, this very briefly summarizes the structure and operations of the brain and how they contribute to the unique experiences that each of us has.

Brain Flexibility

Plasticity is another feature of the brain that you should get quite acquainted with. The capacity of the brain to change and develop is known as brain plasticity, sometimes known as neuroplasticity.

It was formerly believed that the brain only developed new neurons and connections during childhood and was permanently fixed after that. However, we now understand that this process is essential to our brains and lasts until death. Although it slows down a little in adulthood, it allows us to learn, alter our opinions, and pick up new abilities.

Practice, repetition, and experiences that we consider significant cause neural plasticity. According to the adage "what fires together, wires together," neuroscientists. In other words, a neuron will light up if you had an experience. Two neurons, or more likely two groups of tens of thousands of neurons, may light up if you perceive that item and something else at the exact moment.

You will start to link those two things if you often experience them together. Then, via a process known as myelination, during which the dendrites and axons become insulated to better channel the flow of electricity, that link will get stronger. One neuron will eventually trigger the other neuron's activity. This is how you can remember words in a new language or master complicated dance moves.

How to Control Your Performance by Hacking Your Brain

Although it may seem like a lot to process, maybe you now have a general understanding of how your brain works in some respects. I hope that some of this was fascinating to you as well. After all, it's important to us all!

How can you truly utilize this knowledge constructively is the issue that now arises?

Management of Neurotransmitters

By manipulating the synthesis of certain brain chemicals, you may increase your brain's efficiency, pleasure, or any other desired outcome. Neurotransmitters. We now know that these affect our mood and capacity for learning, so altering the balance of these compounds might be highly beneficial.

This is why the concept of "nootropics" has

attracted much attention. Nootropics are considered "smart drugs" because they may change how neurotransmitters are made, resulting in higher levels of motivational dopamine or lower levels of stress-inducing cortisol. Modafinil changes orexin production, which may radically disrupt our sleep/wake cycle and cause us to feel more alert during the day. Caffeine does the same by eliminating (or, more precisely, neutralizing) the inhibitory neurotransmitter adenosine.

The issue with this approach is that it forces the brain into an unnatural state and makes it difficult to quickly "switch modes." No one brain state is preferable to the others; for instance, calm, not stimulation, is needed for creativity.

Even worse, the brain may adjust to such changes by making us more or less sensitive to the offending neurotransmitters by producing more or fewer "receptor sites" (the locations where the function of the neurotransmitter is). Addiction may potentially result from this.

Although certain neurotransmitters function better when emphasizing neuroplasticity or energy generation, this is often not the answer.

A far more practical approach is considering the

variables that naturally affect neurotransmitter release. Examining the inputs is the solution if you want to hack any system.

We thus know that strong light may boost our energy and prevent us from falling asleep, so why not consider investing in a daylight lamp that simulates the sun's rays to treat SAD (Seasonal Affective Disorder)? We know that heat may make us feel more content and relaxed, while cold can help us concentrate. We are aware that the creation of serotonin by the sun and exercise might improve our mood.

We also know that our brain experiences regular natural cycles, such as those related to appetite and sleep. We can work more efficiently and without as many distractions if we schedule our productivity around such things.

And it may be worthwhile to consider some of the biological aspects that might be the root of your extreme stress or depression. Maybe you're hungry? The pro-inflammatory cytokines may also contribute to mild illness and produce cognitive fog.

Since the issue is temporary and biological, letting it go may be considerably simpler.

Controlling Your Brain

But more significantly, you must learn to utilize your brain and alter your thinking to generate your desired emotions and experiences.

The capacity to visualize—to absorb experiences and conjure up hypothetical futures—distinguishes humans from other animals. This is our working memory in action, which permits us to consider long-term objectives and develop original ideas. Furthermore, if you accept the 'embodied cognition' notion, you could discover that this is how we even comprehend everyday English (do some research on it; it's fantastic!).

When we picture or imagine something, our brains activate the same neurons as if the event were occurring. From a neurological perspective, we can hardly distinguish between doing something and imagining it.

As a result, you may use visualization to exercise skills and build knowledge, and cause brain plasticity to occur exactly as if you were performing the task at hand. Additionally, you may utilize this to activate the proper neurotransmitters and put yourself in the appropriate frame of mind.

This will eventually result in the capacity to manage your own emotions.

To induce the most suitable frame of mind for the work at hand. It takes practice to develop your visualization abilities and the knowledge to know when to use them to reduce tension and inspire yourself to concentrate and become more attentive when it's called for. This is the neurobiology that underpins ideologies like stoicism as well as psychological techniques like cognitive behavioral therapy.

This is another reason it's crucial to avoid negative habits, including poor habits of the mind, since brooding and overindulging establish connections that make it more difficult to break harmful habits.

Making the most of your brain involves much more, but I hope this fundamental introduction has helped you get better knowledge and a little more control.

Chapter 9
Setting Goals Made Easy

You must first identify what you want out of life to achieve it. How can you reach your potential if you don't know who you are or what makes you happy?

Because of this, creating goals is a skill that should be cultivated and that everyone should put more effort into acquiring. Living becomes akin to embarking on a trip without end if you are unsure of your aims. Even if you follow the shortest path possible throughout the travel, you risk being somewhere you don't want to be.

So, it must be easy, right? Simply ask yourself what you want from life, and then take action to get it. Right?

Regrettably, no. Setting goals is, unfortunately, not simple and requires a lot of expertise. The issue is that few individuals are aware of this and, therefore, never consider evaluating the objectives' effectiveness on their own. They place blame on their drive, their environment, or even other individuals.

However, they rarely consider the possibility that the error may be in the objective.

You will learn what constitutes a great objective in this tutorial and how to create goals and targets you have a high chance of achieving. After you're done, you may understand why things in your life haven't yet gone according to plan.

An Example Of Poor Goal-Setting

It might be useful first to consider what creates a terrible goal to comprehend how to develop a good goal. Why is it that certain objectives just don't pan out as they ought to? What should we do to prevent this from occurring again?

Consider for a minute that you wish to lose weight. You want to gain muscle and lose weight, which is a relatively common objective that many people are considering achieving.

In this situation, a common objective may include jotting down the desired weights and/or dimensions you're attempting to achieve and then establishing a target for 3 months, 6 months, or 1 year for yourself. Then you start doing it!

However, this is an impossible objective. Why? Because it is just too nebulous, far away, and beyond your control.

Let's skip forward two weeks, by which time you should have been working out regularly and making dietary changes. Life begins to obstruct us all of a sudden. You find yourself overloaded with other responsibilities and lack the time and energy to go to the gym today. or the next day. And Wednesday seems to be difficult. Thursday is also.

But it's OK. since you are not required to exercise. Your objective is not broken if you choose not to exercise on certain days. It is up to you how you will achieve your objective; you have plenty of time to do so. Therefore, if you take today off, you'll make up for it tomorrow. or the next day. If this week is a bust, there's always next week to make up for it.

Week after week, it goes on like this until you reach the end of the time given and realize you have little hope of achieving your objective.

Or how about trying this other scenario? Imagine that you made an effort to become in shape by putting in the necessary time and daily effort. But the weight simply wouldn't go away. Perhaps you have a sluggish metabolism, or too many people ask to take you to supper.

In any case, you reach a certain point and acknowledge again that you won't succeed even though you made an effort.

What do you do then? Disappointed, you give up and wait a long time before you attempt again.

Better Goal

Let's assume an identical situation, but this time appropriately state the aim. What would a decent objective look like if you wanted to gain muscle and decrease weight?

You should start by removing the time component. Why not strive to achieve something every day rather than complete something in X number of days? Look at the objective you want to achieve, and then divide it into much more manageable chunks. You must consume no more than 2,000 calories each day if you want to reduce weight. Additionally, you must exercise three times every week.

If you are able to accomplish that, changes—no

matter how small—will ultimately become apparent.

So choose a short-term objective for yourself instead of concentrating on the eventual result. Since you have complete control over this, you cannot 'fail' due to circumstances outside your control. Additionally, it is resistant to being postponed or delayed. You can't 'work out now' and then work out tomorrow! A sluggish metabolism won't stop you from consuming merely 2,000 calories.

Jerry Seinfeld describes a strategy he utilizes to ensure he adheres to the objectives he refers to as "the chain." The concept is that when he meets his daily goals, a chain forms, which puts enormous pressure on him to keep the link intact.

This may be accomplished with a calendar and a pen. So, you mark the calendar with a checkmark for each day that you exercise effectively. This will eventually result in a row of ticks that you will gradually begin to feel proud of and won't want to spoil by missing one. 'Breaking the chain' is not something you'll want to do.

Whether or whether you want to employ this extra tactic, the key is to create short-term, straightforward objectives. In the meantime, you may let the main goal "take care of itself."

Is Your Goal Too Ambitious?

An ambitious goal is quite acceptable. Many claims that "dreaming big" might even increase your chances of success since it grabs attention, draws others to you, and helps get support. People will respond to your desire to go to space far more favorably than you would to your desire to scale Wales' Mount Snowdown, which is a low peak.

Because of this, another piece of advice often given is to "have visions, not goals." Visions are expansive and ethereal. Instead of being items you list and check off, they are things you see in your head and dream about. If you want to be in shape, your objective can be to go out three times per week, but your ultimate aim should be to achieve the finest possible physical specimen—someone who is confident, attractive, and full of energy.

However, even if a vision might be as expansive and dramatic as you wish, the lesser stages should still be manageable. These stages should be simple, at least initially, allowing you to progress toward your larger, more general goal. Consider it as a hierarchy. Your big vision for the future is at the top; it's something so thrilling that it motivates you to get out of bed in the morning.

Below, you may put your "realistic" assessment of what you can do in light of your available resources. You may have the daily actions you're doing to get there below it.

The error that many individuals make is to group all of these things without considering how one must go from one level to the next. This is the reason a person who has never worked out in a gym may readily develop a new training program for oneself that calls for them to work out for an hour a day, seven days a week, while maintaining a diet of 1,000 calories.

Following that, they'll do some stretching before beginning a yoga lesson.

Is it surprising that we don't always adhere to these objectives?

The root of the issue is usually impatience. People desire to reach their objectives right away. They are unwilling to put in the time or perform the tedious effort necessary to reach that stage. Additionally, they don't want the risk that their efforts may not be worthwhile.

But you must alter that way of thinking. Everything worth having requires labor and devotion, which are sometimes terribly monotonous and uninteresting. It takes years to reach the point where your new body is stunning and "permanent" If you want to become in shape, you must work out often. You need to understand a lot before starting a company if you want to launch one. (Procrastinating on a goal is just as awful, which is another reason you must have a clear action plan!)

Imagine this as a video game. Computer games must start with a few absurdly simple levels to stop you as the player from furiously leaving. Your objectives should be the same; otherwise, you won't succeed. For example, if your "level one" is a huge boss encounter.

When running for the first time, many individuals do this incorrectly. Here, people want to start shedding weight and jogging for big distances straight soon. They are left breathless and sore for days following it because it is exhausting, uncomfortable, and unrewarding.

They should put their first emphasis on improving their running and developing a love for it.

As a result, they should run only short distances,

avoid running too quickly or long, and avoid exerting themselves beyond what is reasonable. In this manner, youngsters might gradually develop a liking for running and discover that they can go further without even attempting it.

In truth, getting where you want to go typically only requires tiny modifications. The Japanese concept of "Kaizen" is the greatest illustration of this. Kaizen is a Japanese term that basically means "many small changes that add up to big results."

For instance, it could be simpler to focus on minor adjustments you can do to get there rather than major ones if you want to lose weight:

On your commute, walk from the bus stop to your final destination. The morning cup of caloric coffee should be avoided.

- As your primary source of hydration, swap sugary soda drinks for still water.
- Your lunchbox and remove your snack.
- Consume from smaller plates.

These are just a few tiny adjustments that most individuals should find simple. Still, they may be sufficient to significantly tilt your calorie total in your favor, ultimately resulting in cumulative weight reduction!

Concluding Remarks

As you can see, understanding how to frame your objectives properly may significantly impact your chance of achieving them. Setting big goals yet having specific, manageable measures you may take along the road to get there is essential. Forget about how long it will take, accept that it will be "boring," and simply concentrate on doing the same few things every day until you ultimately accomplish what you want to do or transform into the person you want to become.

What happens if you evaluate the issue a year from now and still haven't achieved the desired progress? Then maybe you should revisit those objectives. This requires time, effort, and practice, just like everything else. But you're not rushing at all!

Chapter 10
Clear Your Mind

Your mental clarity and self-control capacity determine your experience and quality of life.

Many think the outside world influences our happiness and what happens to us. However, this is untrue.

Instead, how we respond to what happens determines how happy we are. The same holds for every other part of our existence: your stress levels are a function of how you respond to situations, and your capacity for productivity also depends on how you respond.

Don't you trust me? Consider yourself in a caravan perched precariously on the brink of a cliff to illustrate the point. If you move too much, it will fall over the cliff and into a ravine.

If you know this circumstance, you almost certainly feel paralyzed by terror. Your blood vessels will enlarge, your heart rate will rise, your muscles will tighten, and your respiration will become rapid. You'll sweat, and your thoughts will be scattered.

Imagine, however, if you are in the same circumstance but believe you can fly. If so, you'll probably read contentedly while sitting there without giving your perilous posture any thought.

As you can see, not only is your belief about the circumstances and the events controlling your mood, but also your basic physiology. And who do you think has a better chance of escaping this circumstance unscathed without causing the caravan to collapse?

Understand me, though: I'm not trying to convince you that having entirely irrational thoughts is the best course of action! Neither should you delude yourself into thinking you can fly.

But this is only an example of the mind's and your beliefs' strength. If you put yourself in a different, more practical situation, you can see how your beliefs may alter your behavior.

Imagine you are ready to deliver a speech in front of a large audience while standing on stage.

Some of us doubt our ability to fly. Some of us worry that we'll say something stupid, stammer, and that others will laugh at us. As a result, we start to panic, and guess what? Our pulse rate increases, our blood vessels widen, and our muscles tighten. Our mouth is dry and hoarse, and our mind starts to run, increasing our tendency to make errors. The irony is that since we're scared it could, the speech is far more likely to go wrong!

Imagine the same situation, but you are certain it will succeed this time, or you just don't care what others may think. You may behave as if there isn't even an audience by maintaining this level of peaceful awareness.

Once again, how you respond to the situation will determine how much stress you experience.

Additionally, mindfulness and composure are useful in circumstances other than very stressful ones. Imagine, for instance, that when you go home from work, you are consumed with thoughts about what your employer, customer, or colleague recently said to you. You then doubt if you sent that crucial final email.

When you go home, how attentive will you be? How much will your family likely like your company?

Imagine yourself enjoying a wonderful vacation, but all you can worry about is whether you turned on the oven at home. How much do you anticipate savoring the breathtaking mountain views outside your window?

Think about working out at the gym while thinking about the video game you played the night before or X Factor. Do you honestly believe you will be able to use your utmost amount of force throughout that workout?

CBT introduction

Our goal is to assist you in regaining control of your mind, and in doing so, you will also regain control of your emotions and feelings.

The final consequence is that you will eventually be able to stop paying attention to harmful worries, anxieties, and emotions to be fully present and "mindful" at any given time.

CBT is a psychological school that may assist us in achieving this. Cognitive behavioral therapy, or CBT, aims to give you more control over your ideas. Additionally, CBT begins with a kind of mindfulness meditation.

Being more conscious of your own thoughts and

emotions when you meditate is known as mindfulness meditation. In addition to these types of meditation, there is transcendental meditation.

Ask the user to make every effort to thoroughly clear their mind, often by concentrating on a single point in space or possibly a sound or phrase (this is known as a "mantra" and is why we picture Buddhist monks humming while they meditate!). With mindfulness, on the other hand, your goal is to just 'see them' as they pass through you rather than attempting to banish them entirely. The concept is that you are becoming aware of the thoughts you often have but aren't conversing with them or acting on them.

Allow them to influence you. It is often said that you should observe them as they pass by "like clouds in the sky."

After some time, continue doing this, and then jot down some of your ideas. Look at the issues you often worry and stress about, and think about them objectively and detachedly without passing judgment.

Behavioral Restructuring

The CBT expert would next give you instructions to start dissecting and analyzing those ideas. Some of them will be issues that you will be fretting and thinking about, preventing you from fully appreciating the present.

You'll practice rejecting them, but to aid in the process, you'll also take them apart utilizing restructuring methods.

'Thought challenging' is one method for doing this, and it teaches you to question the integrity of your concerns or diversions.

Let's take the scenario where you are concerned about failing to send an email at work. You can get through this by confronting your thoughts. You start by considering if you have any options. What good does worrying serve if that is the case? What is more,

You must unwind and have fun to face the difficulties tomorrow, feeling good and refreshed.

Then you inquire as to its actual significance. What could go wrong? Everyone makes errors, so your manager probably won't be angry with you; instead, they'll be sympathetic.

Do you even somewhat suspect that you'll lose your job? Then just keep in mind that it would be far more difficult for a company to accomplish this lawfully than for you.

Furthermore, would you want to work at a location where you may be fired so easily?

Are you concerned that others may be angry with you? You erred, of course! Then what? And when did you start needing to be best friends with your coworkers?

When you can learn to deconstruct your problems this way, it will be easier to just forget about them and resume enjoying whatever you're doing—or maintaining your composure under pressure.

How to Use The Body Scan Meditation

One of the most significant methods to encourage awareness, serenity, and self-control is meditation.

Tim Ferriss examines the routines and habits of the most successful individuals in the world in his book Tools of Titans. He discovers that they have some similarities, and one of these similarities is that they all meditate.

Everyone, even Tony Robbins, Elon Musk, and Arnold Schwarzenegger, credit meditation as a crucial element for their success.

You may learn to ignore your problems and "be" while meditating. But more significantly, you increase your ability to focus and concentrate, which will keep your mind from being too nervous in the first place.

How, then, do you start to meditate?

Start with the body scan approach as a good tactic. Cross your legs and sit down comfortably. Place your hands on your knees to begin. Maintain a straight back, a forward-facing chin, and closed eyelids, but avoid putting yourself in a position where you could nod off.

Simply'scan' your body by concentrating on each component, noting how it feels, and then relaxing it. But first, you start with your senses. Pay close attention to your surroundings. You'll discover that there are noises you had previously entirely tuned out, and you'll hear the wind howling, children playing, and birds chirping.

Consider your skin's warmth if you're on a tiny incline and how the light moves through your eyelashes.

OK, start by concentrating on the top of your head, then move your gaze downward to your cheekbones, jaw, neck, and shoulders. If you pause at each moment, consider how it makes you feel. Do you sense any tension? Do you experience any pain? After letting the muscle relax, continue moving.

You will eventually descend to your very base. Then you may start to focus for a bit of time on your breathing. The proper breathing technique is "belly breathing," which starts with the stomach expanding and eventually filling the lungs. Regular, rhythmic breathing through the parasympathetic nervous system may lower your heart rate and make you feel calmer. Finally, focus on the area below the navel and concentrate there. Your center of gravity is here. Therefore focusing here will help you feel grounded.

You may find that sometimes your mind begins to stray throughout this procedure. When this occurs, don't let it worry you. Just silently push such thoughts away and switch your attention back to the task. It's natural and not the end of the world.

Finally, go through the same process in reverse order to turn everything around. That meditation included a body scan!

This strategy is effective because it compels you to focus on the present and block out distractions. It engages you with your body, physicality, and surroundings, which is more significant. Your senses also become richer and more vivid as you do this.

If you keep honing this ability, eventually, you should reach a point where you can become more conscious and present on command - even while moving and doing other things. That entails just pausing to observe your surroundings for a minute. Taking a moment to hear what you can hear. Correcting your posture, too. It means avoiding being engrossed in your thoughts to the point that you miss out on life or experience continual worry and anxiety.

Once you can accomplish this, nothing will be able to arouse you in the same manner unless you specifically want it to. You may always focus on the present and temporarily set the past and future aside. You may delight in life and savor that beautiful flavor.

While the email remains in your outbox unopened, a

chocolate cookie.

The secret to happiness is that you have the power to respond either positively or negatively. Instead of seeing something as a severe danger, you might choose to see it as a challenge or a humorous blip. But it's also the secret to realizing your maximum potential, allowing you to work harder and accomplish more.

About The Author

Benjamin Brayshaw is a Health and Wellness Practitioner, Chiropractor, Teen Mentor, and Author of books on healing through the ages. He is an American who defines himself as straight. He has a postgraduate degree in sports science. He grew up in a working-class neighborhood. After his mother died when he was young, he was raised by his father. He loves exploring...people, places, words, and truths, and he loves encouraging people toward honesty and toward being their best selves.

Other Books By Benjamin Brayshaw

- Prospect Marketing & Financial Attraction: Attract Customers with the Right Business Marketing Strategies
- Stress Management: Proven Techniques For A Peaceful Life
- POWER OF CRYSTAL HEALING: Complete Guide To Get Started With the Healing Power Of Earth Energies
- Be The Best Version Of Yourself, Change Your Life: A Complete Guide Of Physical, Metal, Psychic, and Self Development
- Healing: Through ages, physical and spiritual healing book.
- Your Journey To Calm Anxiety And Panic Attacks
- THE STRESS SOLUTION: Practical Strategies to Overcome Anxiety and Improve Your Well-Being
- Look Beyond Fear & Be Courageous: 6 Proven Ways To Bring Out Bravery
- Mastering Time Management: Techniques and Strategies for Effective Productivity

One Last Thing...

Dear Reader,

I hope you enjoyed reading this book and found it to be valuable for your needs. As an author, it means a lot to me when readers take the time to leave a review on Amazon. Your feedback not only helps me improve my writing but also helps potential readers decide if this book is right for them.

If you have a few minutes to spare, I would greatly appreciate it if you could leave a review on Amazon. Your honest opinion can help other readers make informed decisions and can make a real difference in the success of this book.

To leave a review, simply search for the book title and my name on Amazon.com, and select the book from the search results. Once you have navigated to the book's page, scroll down to the review section and share your thoughts on the book.

Rest assured that every single review is personally read and appreciated by me. Your feedback is crucial in helping me understand what worked well and what could be improved upon in future editions. Thank you in advance for your support and for taking the time to leave a review.

Best regards,

Benjamin Brayshaw